# POISONOUS ANIMALS

# POISONOUS ANIMALS

By George S. Fichter

Franklin Watts
New York London Toronto Sydney
A First Book 1991

Cover photograph copyright © Jeff Foott Productions

Photographs copyright ©: DRK Photos: pp. 8, 15 (both Belinda Wright), 25 (R.J. Erwin), 31 (Stephen J. Krasemann), 35 (Jeff Britnell), 44, 47 (both Doug Perrine), 51 (Dan Cheatham); Jeff Foott Productions: pp. 12, 19, 21, 23, 28, 43; Comstock Inc.: pp. 17, 33, 53, 56 (all Russ Kinne), 55 (Franklin Viola); Frederick D. Atwood: pp. 39, 41, 50.

Library of Congress Cataloging-in-Publication Data

Fichter, George S.
Poisonous animals / George S. Fichter.
p.   cm.—(A First book)
Includes bibliographical references and index.
Summary: Examines different types of animals that are poisonous,
either through their bite, sting, or touch.
ISBN 0-531-20050-7
1. Poisonous animals—Juvenile literature.  [1. Poisonous
animals.]   I. Title.   II. Series.
QL100.F53   1991
591.6′9—dc20                              91-3794 CIP AC

# CONTENTS

# POISONOUS
## ANIMALS

The king cobra is large, poisonous, and aggressive. When annoyed, it raises the first third of its body as a warning.

# 1
## POISONS
## AND THEIR PURPOSE

A cobra spreads its hood and sways menacingly. A rattlesnake rattles its tail and draws the front of its body into an S shape, telling you it is ready to strike. Other poisonous animals are brightly colored. Most dangerous animals, in fact, do let you know in some way that it is wise to avoid them.

Poisonous animals do not go out of their way to attack people. They try first to escape. They use their *venom,* or poison, as a last resort.

Only a few of the many *species,* or kinds, of animals in the world are poisonous. Some use their poisons primarily to kill or to paralyze their prey. Their venoms may also help them to start digesting their victims. Other poisonous animals use their venoms strictly for defense.

The poisons of most animals are very mild and are generally not harmful to humans. But others can cause great pain and may even result in death. Some venoms may not be terribly painful when injected, but after a period of time, they can paralyze either the heart or the breathing muscles and cause them to stop functioning. Other kinds of venoms that affect the blood and body tissues usually cause intense pain immediately. This is followed by a swelling as the flesh in the wound area is destroyed or digested. But most of these poisons are complex and are made up of some of both basic types of venom.

In this book you will meet a few of the most common and most dangerous poisonous animals in the United States and elsewhere in the world. And although these are fascinating animals to learn about, it is *very important* that you avoid *all* poisonous animals.

# 2
## ANIMALS THAT BITE

Some animals first bite their prey, then release venom into the wounds. The venoms they release come from glands in their jaws. These are the same glands that produce *saliva,* a watery fluid that moistens food and starts its digestion.

The saliva of some shrews, tiny mammals related to moles, is poisonous. To humans, the bites of these shrews are painful but are not dangerous. To the shrew's prey—which may be as large as a mouse but is usually an insect, worm, or some other quite small animal—the venom is powerful enough to slow down its struggling or even to cause death.

The venom of poisonous snakes, lizards, and a few other kinds of animals also comes from specialized salivary glands. About 15 percent of the 2,500 to 3,000 kinds of snakes are poisonous. The venom of most of these snakes is weak, but the venom of others can be

11

deadly. Snakes use their poisons for protection and for getting food. More than 1½ million people are bitten by poisonous snakes every year, and over 30,000 of them actually die.

## COBRAS AND THEIR RELATIVES

A king cobra's venom is powerful enough to kill an elephant. The king cobra does not need a poison this strong for getting its food, however, for it makes its meals of other snakes. A king cobra is the longest of all the poisonous snakes. Although it averages 12 feet (about 3.7 m) or less, it may reach a length of nearly 20 feet (about 6 m). Unlike other cobras, it does not sway its body to follow movements, but follows movements only with its eyes.

King cobras live in India and Southeast Asia. Along with other cobras and their relatives, they belong to a large family of snakes that produce poisons which af-

*A shrew may eat up to twice its weight in insects every day. Here a masked shrew has captured a grasshopper for a meal.*

fect breathing and heartbeat. Most of the members of this family have immovable, medium-length fangs located at the front of their mouths.

In proportion to its length, the Indian or spectacled cobra has the widest hood of all the cobras. As do other cobras, it spreads its hood by lifting extra-long neck ribs that stretch loose folds of skin over them. This is the cobra generally used by snake charmers. A snake charmer sways his body as he plays a flute in front of a snake. With fully a third of its body lifted out of the basket in which it is carried, the snake moves in a mimicking motion. But the snake is not swaying to the music, for like all snakes, it can't hear because a snake doesn't have ears.

The Indian cobra mainly eats rats and mice, and will often enter houses or other buildings in search of these meals. On cool nights it may stretch out on the warm sand of trails, where it is likely to be stepped on. These habits put it in contact with people, and because of this it is responsible for a large percentage of the roughly 15,000 deaths caused by snake bites in India every year.

The ringhal and several other cobras that live in Africa release their venom in an unusual way. At the front of each of their short, tubular fangs is a hole. By contracting muscles around their venom glands, they squirt the poison through these holes. The snakes aim

*A snake charmer in India. The cobras cannot actually hear—they sway to the motion of the snake charmer's flute.*

for their victim's eyes, and at distances of about 4 feet (about 1.2 m) they are deadly accurate. A direct hit can cause temporary blindness—time enough for the cobra to escape or to move in closer for the kill. And when they bite, more venom goes into the wound.

Fastest of all the poisonous snakes are the black mambas that live in tropical Africa. They have been timed at a speedy 7 miles (about 11 km) per hour—about twice the top speed for most snakes. A black mamba usually slithers out of sight hurriedly when approached, but when its territory is invaded and especially during the breeding season, a black mamba becomes very disturbed. At these times it will actually chase anyone who comes close. And like the cobras, it has a strong venom.

Two cobra relatives live in the United States: the eastern coral snake of the Southeast and the Arizona coral snake of the Southwest. Both are slender, shiny, and brightly patterned. Eastern coral snakes may reach a length of 4 feet (about 1.2 m), although most are shorter. Arizona coral snakes never grow longer than 2

*A black mamba can move very quickly on the ground and in trees.*

feet (.6 m). Both of these cobra relatives have a powerful venom. Although about one death every five years is caused by the eastern coral snake, no deaths have been recorded as a result of bites from the Arizona coral snake.

During the day, coral snakes ordinarily stay out of sight under rocks or in ground litter. They come out at night to hunt for food. Coral snakes are not aggressive and often can be handled without causing them to bite—but don't do it! When they do bite, they have trouble getting their small mouths over a broad area, such as a hand or a leg, and also in getting their small fangs into a victim to inject venom.

Both coral snakes in the United States have beautiful bands of black, yellow, and red, and both have black snouts. They are slim-bodied and do not have triangular heads as do rattlesnakes and other vipers, and many kinds of harmless snakes.

## SEA SNAKES

Some fifty different kinds of snakes live in the Pacific and Indian oceans. Sometimes thousands of these snakes swarm on the surface of the sea. Fishermen often find them in their nets. These snakes are extremely docile, but they will bite if they are hit or are harmed in

*An Arizona coral snake usually stays in the rocks during the day and hunts at night.*

some other way. The venom of some sea snakes is ranked with the strongest of all poisonous snakes.

The pelagic sea snake is the sea snake most widely found. Because of its striking yellow underside, it is sometimes called the yellow-bellied sea snake. Rarely more than 3 feet (.9 m) long, it appears occasionally along the western coasts of the Americas but so far has not invaded the Atlantic Ocean.

Like other sea snakes, the pelagic sea snake uses its flat tail like an oar for swimming. Females give birth to their young at sea, as do some of the other sea snakes. Others come ashore to lay eggs, like the sea turtles, and like them, they find it very difficult to crawl on land.

## RATTLESNAKES AND THEIR RELATIVES

Rattlesnakes belong to the family of poisonous snakes called *vipers*. All of the vipers have triangular heads. The large venom glands at the rear on each side of the head cause this shape. Their large fangs are hinged, fitting against the roof of the mouth when it is closed and then lifting when the mouth is opened. The fangs are like hypodermic needles, with venom flowing down their hollow interiors into a bite wound. The venom of vipers affects mostly the blood. The pain is immediate and intense, and the area around the bite quickly becomes swollen and discolored.

*The jaw skeleton of a diamondback rattlesnake
showing its large fangs*

In the viper family, rattlesnakes belong to a group called *pit vipers*. Between the nostril and the eye on each side of the head is a pit with special sensory cells that detect heat. With these unique organs, a rattlesnake can determine, even in the dark, both the direction and the amount of body heat given off by nearby birds, mice, or other warm-blooded animals. They then move in to make their kill.

More than a dozen different kinds of rattlesnakes live in the United States. About 7,000 people are bitten every year, but fewer than 12 die from the bites.

These snakes rattle their tails, and so give a warning before they bite, right? Although this is generally true, if a snake is in a hurry, it may not have time to rattle until after it bites. Or there may be almost no time between the rattle and the bite. Do not count on the rattle as protection from these snakes.

Many snakes, in fact, are nervous and vibrate their tails when they are disturbed. A harmless snake's tail

*A rattlesnake may shake its rattles as a warning of attack. It uses the sensory pit beneath each eye to detect the body heat of its prey.*

shaking against dried leaves can sound almost exactly like a rattlesnake. But only the rattlesnakes carry their rattles with them.

A rattle is made up of dry "buttons" at the tip of the tail. It was once believed that each button represented a year in the snake's life. But usually a new button is formed every time the snake sheds its skin. In warm climates a snake may shed its skin six or more times every year.

The eastern diamondback rattlesnake lives along the Gulf Coast and northward along the Atlantic Coast to North Carolina. The largest of all the rattlesnakes, it can reach a length of 8 feet (about 2.4 m). In the United States, it is responsible for the most deaths from snake bites every year. The smallest of the rattlesnakes is the pygmy rattlesnake, which lives in the moist lowlands of the Southeast and Mexico. Its maximum size is 2.5 feet (.76 m), but most are smaller.

Two pit vipers in the United States do not have rattles. These are the cottonmouth, or water moccasin, and the copperhead.

The cottonmouth population is greatest in the swampy lowlands and waterways of the South. A cottonmouth may grow to more than 6 feet (about 1.8 m) in length, although most are shorter. When this snake opens its mouth, it shows a cottony white interior. This is the snake's warning pose. The cottonmouth is

*The cottonmouth is usually
found in southern swamps.*

easily bothered and causes the death of one person every year in the United States. Its venom is about as strong as a rattlesnake's.

Named for the coppery color of its head, the North American copperhead lives in dry upland areas, often on rocky slopes. More people are bitten by copperheads than by any other poisonous snake in the eastern United States. Copperheads, which seldom grow to more than 4 feet (about 1.2 m) in length, do not have a really strong venom. Deaths from their bites are very rare.

The largest of all the vipers and the second largest of all the poisonous snakes in the world is the bushmaster of Central and South America. Nine feet (2.7 m) is not an unusual length for it, and there are records of bushmasters measuring as long as 12 feet (about 3.7 m). The fangs of a big bushmaster may be more than 1 inch (2.5 cm) long. Like the rattlesnake, the bushmaster vibrates its tail when it is disturbed. But unlike the rattlesnake, it doesn't have rattles. It makes a noise only if its spiny-tipped tail strikes leaves or some other object. Fortunately, the bushmaster is not a common snake—a good thing because this snake does not have a gentle disposition.

The fer-de-lance, or barba amarilla, is found in the tropics of Central and South America. It is also found on many islands in this region. The name *fer-de-lance* refs to the snake's spear-shaped head. *Barba amarilla* means "yellow beard," and the snake does have a yellow chin. Reaching a maximum length of 8 feet (about 2.4 m), the fer-de-lance has a brightly colored tail. This attracts the attention of its prey while the snake moves its head into a striking position. The fer-de-lance makes its meals mainly of rats, and for this reason, it has been brought into areas where it did not occur naturally. But it may soon become abundant wherever it goes, because a female fer-de-lance gives birth to thirty or more young in each litter.

Sluggish and brightly colored, the heavy-bodied gaboon viper of Africa's tropical forests holds the record among snakes for having the largest fangs. These fangs may be as much as 2 inches (5.08 cm) long. The gaboon viper's venom is very strong, but this snake is slow to attack. And although the gaboon viper will sometimes grow to 8 feet (about 2.4 m) in length, it usually measures only about 5 feet (about 1.5 m) long.

## LIZARDS

The Gila monster of the southwestern United States and northern Mexico and the closely related beaded lizard found only in Mexico are the only poisonous lizards in the world. Neither of these is common. And

*The Gila monster is one of only two poisonous
lizards in the world. Gila monsters move very
slowly, so it is easy to stay out of their way.*

because it is threatened with extinction, the Gila monster is now protected by law.

These lizards first try to escape. They usually move very slowly, but in emergencies they can travel surprisingly fast. If picked up, they will snap viciously. And when their broad, strong jaws clamp onto a victim, the grip is like a vise.

Fangs? These lizards do not have them. Like snakes, their venom is secreted by enlarged salivary glands, but in these lizards, the venom comes only from glands in their lower jaw. There is no direct connection between the glands and the teeth as there is in snakes. And, unlike snakes, more than half a dozen teeth in both the upper and lower jaws are grooved. The venom flows along these grooves into the bite wound as the lizard chews. This is not a good way to inject poison, of course. The lizards are most successful if they roll onto their backs so the venom flows downward into their prey. A bite from one of these lizards is very painful, but deaths are rare.

The Gila monster measures a little more than 1.5 feet (about .5 m) long, but the beaded lizard may be nearly 3 feet (about .9 m) long. Both use the powerful claws on their short legs for digging, and their thick tail is a reserve of food that they use during hibernation. Their scales are beadlike and are in rows that align both crosswise and diagonally.

All spiders have sharp fangs, and they produce a venom that is used either to kill or subdue their prey. In some spiders, the venom is powerful enough to be dangerous to humans. However, spiders do not attack humans— they bite only to defend themselves.

Four species of widow spiders live in the United States, but only the bite of the female black widow may be deadly. The males do not bite. The female black widow is a shiny black, with a red hourglass mark on the underside of her abdomen. Her venom is a strong nerve poison that may be only mildly painful at first. But it may later cause cramps, nausea, and shock. About 5 percent of the people bitten by the female black widow die.

The brown recluse spider that lives in much of the

*The female black widow spider spins a small, tangled web. You can clearly see the red hourglass mark on the underside of this spider.*

southern United States is probably responsible for many more bites than the black widow. Fortunately, though, its venom is not as strong. The brown recluse looks like any ordinary brown spider, but if you look closely, you will see a dark fiddle-shaped mark on its back. The brown recluse likes living in houses and other buildings. This increases the chances of its being contacted, and it will bite to defend itself. A big red area develops around the bite wound, and healing generally takes several months.

The spiders most commonly referred to as tarantulas belong to a group native mainly to the American tropics, although some kinds live in the southwestern United States. These are huge spiders—one South American species is nearly 4 inches (10 cm) long and has a leg span of about 10 inches (25.4 cm). They are also called bird spiders because they capture and feed on birds, lizards, and other fairly large animals. They hunt for their prey on the ground and usually do their prowling at night.

These giant spiders are sometimes kept as pets. They are typically gentle and seem to like attention. Most are not dangerously poisonous, but they do inject a venom into their bites. And the easily shed hairs on their bodies produce an irritating, stinging sensation when they touch the skin.

*Tarantulas are giant spiders. Their venom is usually harmless to humans. Most tarantulas make their home in ground burrows lined with silk.*

Cone shells are sea or marine snails. Their shells are among the most beautiful and most sought after by shell collectors. Nearly all of the about five hundred kinds of cone shells live in the Pacific and Indian oceans. One kind is found off the coast of California and about a dozen are found in the warm waters of the Gulf of Mexico and the Atlantic off the southern United States. All produce a venom. Only a few—all of them from the Indo-Pacific region—are ranked as really dangerous to humans, but for safety, any living cone shell must be treated with great caution.

Do they bite? They don't really have teeth, but they do have rows of sharp "harpoons" along their tongues. When a cone shell is attacking its prey or defending itself, one or more of these harpoons is pushed into its victim. At the base of each harpoon is a sac containing poison. When the muscles around the sac are squeezed, the venom flows down the hollow harpoon into the wound. The strongest venom can cause death very quickly by paralyzing the heart muscle.

## OCTOPUSES

An octopus is related to clams, snails, and oysters. But unlike these animals, the octopus does not have a shell. Octopuses live in the sea, the largest of them in the

34

*A young giant Pacific octopus skims the
bottom as it looks for food.*

cooler sea waters. An octopus crawls slowly along the ocean bottom or can swim swiftly, propelling itself with a jet of water that shoots out of its body. An octopus does this by drawing water in and then shooting it out through a tube that extends from the rear of its body.

The octopus has eight tentacles, or "arms," that stretch out from its soft, round body. These arms are equipped with suction cups that enable the octopus to hold its prey. The octopus then moves the victim to its mouth. There, its prey is bitten with its sharp beak—like a parrot's—and swallowed. Some octopuses can inject a venom into the bite wound, which slows down or kills their struggling catches. This poison is powerful and takes effect quickly. An Australian octopus with tentacles only 6 inches (15 cm) long is known to have caused one person's death.

# 3

## ANIMALS THAT STING

### BEES AND WASPS

More than a million species of insects have been identified and named. A typical insect has three pairs of legs and two pairs of wings. Some insects, like bees and wasps, also have stingers at the rear of their bodies.

The stings of bees and wasps kill at least two dozen people every year in the United States, twice as many as snakes kill. In some cases, the deaths are caused by many stings, which means that a large amount of venom is injected. These attacks occur when people disturb their nests and cannot get away before many of the insects swarm over them. Most deaths, however, are due to an allergic reaction to the venom. They occur quickly—often as quickly as a minute after the sting.

Because people have more contact with them, honeybees are responsible for most stings. The honeybee's stinger is barbed, and with its attached poison sac, gets stuck in its prey's body. This pulls it out of the bee's body, and the bee then dies.

Bumblebees and wasps do not have barbs on their stingers, and so they can sting many times. With each sting, a small amount of venom is injected into the stab wound. Some wasps have a sting that paralyzes their prey. They then lay their eggs on the victim after it is tucked into a burrow or a mud nest. Their larvae that hatch from the eggs are provided in this way with fresh, living food.

## ANTS

Ants belong to the same group of insects as bees and wasps, and some of them have stingers, too. They use their stingers to protect themselves and their colonies. The stings of ants are extremely painful and can be dangerous if there are a lot of them or there is an allergic reaction.

The most painful stings are from the tropical fire ant. This ant was accidentally introduced into the United States from Brazil and has since spread over much of the South. Fire ants make mounds as much as 3 feet (.9 m) high and 3 feet (.9 m) wide. Each fire ant colony houses hundreds of thousands of ants that look for food over a wide area around the mound. And, unfortunately, it's easy to provoke them to sting.

Bees collect pollen to feed their young. The pollen, mixed with honey produced by the bee, is formed into pellets and stored in the hive.

Below: some wasps make their nests of paperlike material. The nest is divided into cells, and the queen wasp deposits an egg in each cell.

Stinging poisons are produced by the caterpillars of many kinds of butterflies and moths. These poisons are found on the hairs of caterpillars' bodies and are a way that the insect defends itself. This defensive mechanism keeps the caterpillars from being eaten by other animals. When the poison touches human skin, it causes a burning feeling and sometimes a long-lasting rash. Deaths have occurred, probably because of allergic reactions. Caterpillars—especially the hairy ones—should be avoided.

Some other insects give off smelly or stinging body fluids. These may be released when the insect is handled or may be sprayed on an attacker. One of these insects, the bombardier beetle, lifts the tip of its abdomen and lets loose a spray of chemicals that can cause blisters on the skin. If this fluid is rubbed from the hands into the eyes, it can cause temporary blindness.

## SCORPIONS

Scorpions are distinguished from insects by having four pairs of legs rather than three, and by not having wings. They are most closely related to spiders.

All of the more than a thousand species of scorpions have huge pincers, or claws, on front legs like box-

*This woolly bear caterpillar will combine
its spiny hairs with a few strands of silk
to form a cocoon. Eventually the woolly
bear will become a tiger moth.*

ing gloves. The scorpion's long, slim tail is carried curved over its back. Males have bigger pincers and longer tails than females. At the end of the tail is a stinger connected to a round venom sac. The stings of scorpions are painful and feel like a bee sting. But in only a few kinds of scorpions is the venom really dangerous.

Most scorpions live in warm, dry climates like that of the American Southwest. They are active mainly at night, when they hunt for spiders, cockroaches, and other small animals that they can catch in their pincers. Their sting paralyzes their prey.

## JELLYFISH

Jellyfish are well named, because they are made up of a bell-shaped glob of a substance like jelly. Threadlike tentacles hang from this body. In some kinds of jellyfish, these tentacles may stretch to more than 100 feet (30.5 m) from the bell.

Each of these tentacles contains thousands of stinging cells called *nematocysts*. These cells send out tiny harpoons when touched, or even when stimulated by a shift in the water's current. A single stinging cell does not contain enough venom to be harmful or even to be noticed. But if several tentacles are involved, thousands

*The Giant Desert Hairy Scorpion is at home in the Mojave desert.*

of these little cells release their harpoons. Then the amount of venom released can be very large.

Venom from most kinds of jellyfish only causes a stinging. But sea wasps, jellyfish that live in the Pacific from Japan to Australia, produce such a powerful venom that these animals are among the most dangerous in the sea. Sea wasps belong to a group called box jellies because their "bells" are four-sided, or nearly square. Their tentacles hang in clusters at each of the four corners of their bodies.

Because they are nearly transparent, as are all jellyfish, sea wasps are difficult to see in the water. They do not attack, but when currents carry them into the shallows along beaches, their tentacles may come into contact with an object. The stinging cells are then automatically discharged. On a crowded beach, this can be disastrous. A sea wasp's stings may cause death in less than a minute.

*A typical jellyfish with many threadlike tentacles around the edge of its body*

Beaches along the lower southeastern coast of the United States are closed to swimmers when winds and currents bring fleets of the Portuguese man-of-war toward shore.

A Portuguese man-of-war is related to the jellyfish, but it is not a single animal. It is a colony of individuals, each performing different functions that contribute to the survival of the group. A part of the colony is a purplish, gas-filled, sausage-shaped float with an orange-red crest. The float may be nearly 12 inches (.3 m) long. Hanging from it is a curtain of tentacles. Stretched out, each tentacle may be 20 feet (about 6 m) long, occasionally twice as long.

When a tentacle touches something, its stinging cells are discharged. Tiny crustaceans, or other small animals on which the Portuguese man-of-war feeds, are drawn into the center of the colony and are absorbed. When washed on shore with their tentacles stretched out over the sand, these unusual animals can be dangerous to people. A single stinging cell contains only a tiny amount of venom, but the poison is very strong. Chemically, it is a lot like cobra venom. Because a Portuguese man-of-war may have 500,000 or more stinging cells in each tentacle, one or more of the tentacles can send out thousands of these deadly little darts. The

46

*A Portuguese man-of-war is really a colony
of individual animals. Each tentacle has many
stinging cells containing very strong venom.*

immediate effect is like being stung by a lot of bees—an intense and shocking pain. This may be followed by stomach cramps and dizziness.

The ability to sting protects the Portuguese man-of-war from most other creatures in the sea. One little fish, however, lives among the tentacles, darting out to get its meals and then retreating back to where it is safe from predators. This fish, the man-of-war fish, is not immune to the venom. It must be very careful to avoid stings. Another animal, the loggerhead turtle, does seem to have an immunity, and regularly makes its meals of these strange man-of-war animals.

# 4

## ANIMALS DANGEROUS TO TOUCH

### AMPHIBIANS

Frogs, toads, salamanders, and newts—these are amphibians. They form a group of animals that spend part of their lives in water and part on land. During the stage of their lives when they live on land, their skin is kept moist by secretions from glands scattered over its surface. Sometimes they are clumped into bumps or warts. In most amphibians, these secretions are at least mildly poisonous, and in some they are very strong. This protects the animals from would-be predators.

The venom from one poison dart or arrow frog in Colombia can kill more than 15,000 mice. Like many poisonous animals, these frogs are brightly colored— an advertisement that they are dangerous. Indians living in this region rub the points of darts used in their blowguns over a frog's skin to pick up enough venom

*The skin of these brightly colored poison
arrow frogs secretes a strong poison.*

*Yagua Indians show how they shoot poison darts.*
*The points of the darts have been rubbed on the*
*skin of the poison arrow frog.*

to kill whatever the dart strikes. They also roast the frogs on sticks and then collect the poisonous secretions that are cooked out of its skin.

Another very dangerous amphibian is the marine toad. Its skin secretions are strong enough to kill a dog. If people get some of the secretion on their hands and then rub their eyes, they will be temporarily blinded. A native of South America, this big toad—up to 9 inches (22.8 cm) long—has been shipped around the world to help control insects that damage vegetable crops. It was introduced to the United States accidentally, when a shipping crate was broken at Miami International Airport and the toads inside made their escape.

Also very poisonous in the United States is the Colorado river toad. Like the marine toad's poison, its poison is produced by two large kidney-shaped glands, one behind each eye, and also in many small, warty bumps scattered over its body.

## SCORPION FISH

Fish are the most abundant of the vertebrates, or animals with backbones. There are more than 40,000 different kinds of fish. More than 300 species make up the scorpion fish family, which includes the spiniest and most poisonous fish in the world. The most venomous of these are the several species of stonefish that live in

A Colorado river toad has a large poison
gland behind each eye.

shallow Indo-Pacific waters. Their flat, "warty" bodies, most less than 12 inches (.3 m) long, are perfect camouflage among the rocks where they live. Their venom is produced in glands at the base of the stout first spines in their fins. If a fish is grabbed so that a spine causes a puncture wound, venom flows down the spine into the opening.

## CATFISH

Catfish live primarily in ponds, lakes, and streams, but a few species are found in the sea. Most kinds do not have scales or armor, and usually have a sharp spine in each of the side fins and also in the high fin on their back. Some have venom glands at the base of these spines. Stab wounds from these spines are painful and heal slowly.

$$\ast \qquad \ast \qquad \ast$$

Remember that poisonous animals are not creatures with a mission to harm or to kill people. Their venom serves them either for getting food or for defense.

Because many of them can kill or can at least cause great pain and discomfort, you should be careful around them. Let them go on their way without bothering them.

Accidents may happen, however. If you are bitten

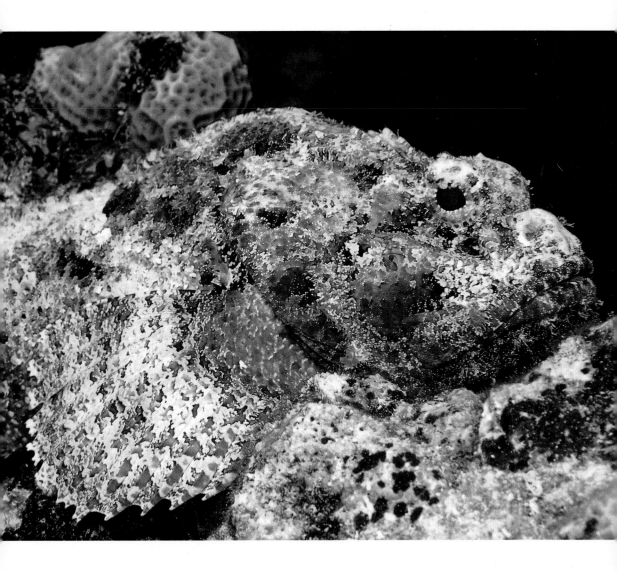

*The poisonous spotted scorpion fish
has such excellent camouflage it is hard
to spot among the rocks where it lives.*

*A shovelnosed catfish. Most of
the commercially available catfish in the
United States are raised on fish farms.*

or stung, get medical attention as quickly as possible. Be prepared to tell what kind of animal has bitten or stung you so that you can get the proper treatment.

The chances of any poisonous animal giving you serious difficulty are very small, however. This is especially true if you are watchful, careful, and cautious where these animals live.

# FOR FURTHER READING

Arehart-Treckel, Joan. *Poisons and Toxins*. New York: Holiday House, 1976.

Bender, Lionel. *Poisonous Insects*. New York: Gloucester Press, 1988.

Freedman, Russell. *Killer Snakes*. New York: Holiday House, 1982.

Gadd, Lawrence. *Deadly Beautiful: The World's Most Poisonous Animals and Plants*. New York: Macmillan, 1980.

Haines, Gail Kay. *Natural and Synthetic Poisons*. New York: William Morrow, 1978.

Hellman, Hal. *Deadly Bugs and Killer Insects*. New York: M. Evans and Company, Inc., 1978.

McCarthy, Colin. *Poisonous Snakes*. New York: Gloucester Press, 1987.

Phelps, Tony. *Poisonous Snakes*. Poole, Dorset, England: Blandford Press, 1981.

# INDEX

# ABOUT THE AUTHOR

George S. Fichter is a widely published author of books and articles, including many for young people. He has written several books for Franklin Watts, among them the recently revised First Book *The Space Shuttle*.

Mr. Fichter has spent most of his career as a freelance author and editor. He lives in Florida where, on occasion, he may encounter some of the animals described in this book.